Helen,

I hope we get to meet each other soon.

Thank you for reading & sipping along.

Kitty

Coffee Life Thoughts...One Cup at a time

Written by

Kitty Shields

Illustrations by

Jon Ross Shields

Coffee Life Thoughts…One Cup at a time

ISBN 978-1506-914-89-3 HCJ
ISBN 978-1506-914-88-6 PBK

Jan 2025

Published and Distributed by
First Edition Design Publishing, Inc.
P.O. Box 17646, Sarasota, FL 34276-3217
www.firsteditiondesignpublishing.com

Table of Cups

Welcome Aboard

GOOD MORNING! THIS IS YOUR WAKE-UP CALL!

Those eight dreaded words, that I heard at the other end of my hotel room phone from extremely cheerful guest receptionists, were my alarm and incentive that I had to get out of my slumber, come alive and move rather quickly to get my workday started. My first thought of the morning after I successfully found the phone to answer, was without a doubt...I NEED COFFEE.

Dragging my feet out of bed, I made a beeline for the electric kettle to fill with water for my much-needed caffeine jolt. The next feat of the morning was to head to the hotel shower once my coffee was prepared and carefully perch my cup on the bathtub edge and drink my hot beverage while showering as I was down to seconds to be punctual for the coach that was my transportation to the airport. Sips and suds took on a whole new meaning for my work mornings, and I was down to time management.

With the second hand of the clock, quickly making its round, it was time to get dressed for the day. Uniform prep with a quick ironing of the blouse or dress, a little make up application, repacking my suitcase, double checking the room to make sure I have all my belongings, ID around my neck and finally, a brisk walk to the elevator, bags in tow, as I made my way to the first floor to meet my fellow friends and colleagues.

I jumped on the coffee drinking train in 1989 when I was hired by Delta Air Lines as a Flight Attendant. Wake up calls could happen as early as 3:00 am and the black hot liquid was a much- welcomed addition to my mornings. Who am I kidding? In my early coffee days, the liquid was extremely light brown and loaded with a cup of sugar. Now that drinking my friend "JOE", has become old hat to me, I prefer it extremely dark and robust. I had a passenger order coffee in the language of Swahili, and I loved their word for it, kahawa. I have enjoyed tasting the different brews from all over the world and it really has become a passion for me.

Along with my past time of partaking in the bean juice, I assembled a collection of mugs. The assortment of cups that are made of pottery, glass and ceramic started from gathering them on my travels from favorite destinations, eating establishments, pubs, gifts from friends with inside jokes or messages, and some I added simply because I admired the style, motif or design. I love seeing so much positivity and items I adore when I pull open the cabinet door that houses my fun vessels.

The daily handpick of my mug is based on different thoughts and feelings that have come about in my mornings or what is going on currently in my life. I could be thinking about or missing a friend, or I want to visit a favorite spot and make as if

I'm being whisked away there for a few hours, maybe someone could use a prayer, or I just want to use an old favorite. Whatever and whomever are on my mind I make my choice, accordingly, fill it to the brim and head to my favorite chair to begin my early morning, reflective readings. There's just something so special about being the only one awake in the house with a cup of coffee and quiet time.

Most of the mugs remind me of something in my life that has happened and almost all of them jog my memory of valuable lessons, fond experiences and life thoughts that I love to think and reflect upon; so much so that I decided to write about them in a collection on pages for fun, that will help me complete a goal and fill up my personal creative cup. Also, these pages allow me to pay homage to my parents, re-learn some very special memories and keep telling their stories.

The most special aspect of this project for me is my son has done the illustrations for each one with his interpretations of my words. We have shared many cups of coffee together over the years and we certainly have in common the love of java beans. Pair that with good conversation and we have the perfect morning blend.

I would be honored if you would take a little journey down memory lane with me. I invite you to sit back and relax, grab a blanket and your cup of Joe. Don your slippers, put your seat back and your tray table down. Let's get ready to take off together with our destinations finding us amongst a few of my favorites from my collection and enjoy COFFEE LIFE THOUGHTS...One Cup at a Time. Thank you for reading and sipping along.

Coffee Across the Miles at MOM's PLACE

I grew up enjoying family meals at a wooden antique kitchen table, with the freshest garden to plate, field to fork dishes that one could imagine. Without a doubt, black coffee was always served with every scrumptious meal and was the beverage of choice for my parents. As a young girl to me it looked like sludge and was unpalatable. I would sample the morning and after dinner coffee occasionally and think there is not a chance that I will ever get to enjoy this beverage that my parents loved/love so much. As much as I wanted to partake in their ritual, it was not happening. Now, thanks to my career path and the need for caffeine, it has become a way of life and a treasured past time for my mom and me.

Anyone that has ever been an overnight guest at my mother's home knows the morning routine after a bit of shut eye. First one to arise for the day, better get coffee brewing as the sleepy heads in the household love to have that Folgers moment of "Best Part of Waking Up" as we hear the trickling of the pot. We all seem to have favorite mugs that we reach for, fill them up and head to the three, vertical, wall size dining room windows to see the many different types of trees and flowers in bloom and visit with the birds, deer, squirrels, chipmunks, rabbits or whatever wildlife is around to wake up and have coffee with them. I always love it when one of my mom's wingback chairs is available. I grab a blanket, put my feet up on a wooden stool and sip the morning brew. The best seat in the house and the house blend that is served is coincidentally FOLGERS, black silk. My Mom is 95 and still living in my childhood home, so coffee mornings are extremely special. During my visits before I find my way to my childhood bedroom that has one of my grand-mothers' handmade quilts on the bed, I kiss my mother good night and wish her sweet dreams and never miss saying, "SEE YOU FOR COFFEE IN THE MORNING MOM".

I'll never forget the day when my parents took me to the airport in Pittsburgh, Pa so that I could board my flight to Atlanta to begin my journey with Delta Air Lines. My 6 weeks of flight attending training was about to commence. I was living at home as I had just graduated from college and my first grown-up job was taking me to The Peach State. The time frame was pre-9-11 and loved ones could escort you to the departure gates. I begged for it not to be my turn to board the metal tube that was waiting for me. I was not ready to leave my parents; my faithful, main source of comfort. No such luck, my dreaded seat row was called, (this was before boarding zones existed) and I had no choice but to hug and say my good-byes and start the trip that seemed like an eternity to my assigned seat. I must've looked back a million times through tears to see my mom and dad. Every glance I would see my best friends waving and love beaming from their sad faces. I vowed right then and there that I would make it a point to see those two amazing human beings somehow, someway every month for the rest of my life. I didn't care if Delta was assigning my new base for work in Tibet, I was getting home to my folks. Southern Asia luckily for me was not my first base assignment, and I did make the monthly sojourn since August

30,1989 only missing 3 times of my once-a-month goal of visiting with my parents or mom.

Recently my mother thanked me for keeping my commitment for over 30 years and was so grateful that I made that promise and did so well at keeping my word. Of course, this conversation took place in front of my favorite dining room windows with sips of coffee.

I get the message loud and clear that time is a thief, and I have unfortunately experienced significant loss of family and friends and that seasons go by in the blink of an eye. Not all of us are gifted the privilege of longevity but while we are on this earth together, our common denominator is time. It's up to us to make the choices and act on how we use our clocks. To me it is worth the effort and sacrifices that it takes to be there for family and friends. Memories stay forever in our hearts and minds and there will be no regrets when time is set aside to be together. Goodbyes are difficult, but the reflection of the minutes spent fills the soul with vitality, vigor and verve.

I believe it is imperative to GO ACROSS THE MILES. Travel by car, bus, train, boat, motorcycle, vespa, bicycle, skateboard and of course plane. Whatever it takes to fit these priceless getaways into our schedules. The investment is worth every penny and the time spent is worth every sip. The flashbacks truly will last a lifetime, and it all seems to come down to geography and maybe adding points to frequent flyer accounts. It is indisputable that we are never promised tomorrow, that I know for sure. Make the time to be together and stay connected, in any way possible, ACROSS THE MILES.

ENJOY THE JOURNEY ...unpacking one cardboard box at a time!

I'd like to pat myself on the back for a second and state that one of my greatest qualities is that I bloom where I am planted. This characteristic has come in handy with my life trajectory or perhaps it's because, sometimes I didn't have a choice and had to do what I had to do. My husband Rustin has chosen a career that presents many changes. The new job variations have brought results that require us to hire different Moving Companies to help us tour around the United States. Moves are right up there with the Top 5 stresses in life. I know. I know all too well. Our relocations can come with steep hills to climb and many hurdles to cross, however we seem to make hay while the sun shines and enjoy our new adventures.

We have lived in Indianapolis, Pittsburgh, Tampa three different times, Buffalo, Greensboro, Siler City, Sandusky, Holland and currently Roanoke. I love finding hidden gems where we land and exploring our newfound territories. At one point on our journey together we were a little overzealous and made three transitions in a years' time frame. A dear friend knew that I needed a little reminder to enjoy my journey and thought this mug and message would be a help. However, my Amiga also taught me a life changing lesson that I would like to model and put into use.

Roanoke Virginia is our latest lifestyle shift, and I found myself knee deep in boxes all over the floors of our city apartment that we purchased. The cardboard nuisances were filled with our belongings from Two homes now combined into one place. There was nowhere to step without jumping over or moving a box. I couldn't seem to get motivated to start the unpacking process. The best thing I could think of doing was to make a video so that my friends could share in the misery. I needed a little rah-rah support! Buds are great at those little ditties! It's like having your own personal built in cheerleading squad waiting on the sidelines with big fluffy pom poms.

Before I could get motivated to use the utility knife that I held in my hand to slice open box after box, I was answering my phone from one of my cheerleaders that just viewed my current fresh hell, stating that she had purchased an airline ticket and is coming to The Star City to be with me and help. "Put me to work Kitten...I'm on my way!" I had to move a box or two after we finished our call to find a seat on the floor to have a good cry. Tears fell because I was exhausted but mostly, they were flowing from knowing how lucky I was to have a drop everything friend that is going to remind me to enjoy my journey. I didn't need to ask anything from this angel, she just went into superpower mode and jumped into action.

I don't know why it is so hard for me to request assistance. It truly is difficult for me to make the ask. I think so many people share my thought and if you don't...good for you.

I learned from this experience to just do it. Jump in at the deep end and swim your way to your loved ones. Take soup, meatballs, chicken salad, pasta, cake, cookies, donuts, cupcakes, brownies, pies, care packages, plants, flowers, iced tea, lemonade, smoothies, banana bread, breakfast croissants; anything you can think of to help someone that may need a boost. Then just sit back and see the smiles. Show up after a party and grab a mop and become the mad mopper or start loading the dishwasher or wash dishes. Check in on a friend's aging parent or parents, visit a friend, book a lunch date, meet for coffee, plan a girl's trip or a night out, bring in empty trash and recycle cans when it's a struggle for someone to complete that chore, mail a card or letter, invite the new kid in town for cocktails or lunch, drive a friend to an appointment or the airport. Give someone a shot of sunshine and reminder to enjoy the journey. JUST go ahead and DO IT. I promise it will feed the soul and leave many hearts gleaming, including your own.

We all deserve to enjoy our journeys. It's wonderful to get by with a little help from our friends, family and angels on earth. It is what makes the world go round and opens hearts one cardboard box at a time.

OUTLOOK MOSTLY SUNNY... SURFS UP

The pandemic of 2020. The world seemed to stop spinning for a bit and we found ourselves in one place with the same walls and in my case the same person, my husband, day in day out. We were in lockdown in Tampa Florida.

Our two ventures out of our home included the allotted jail break for groceries and the panic buying of Charmin at Publix and we also took to the pavement for an exercise regime of walking to enjoy the sunny, clear blue skies. After our health-related activity, we had a time frame that we dubbed the no talking hours until 5:00 o'clock, our daily Happy Hour. We needed a reprieve for personal time and sanity.

During the silent hours, my first past time was calling and checking on my mom, son, brother and friends. I also took this forced time out from life to brush up on my hobbies and interests and get my home organized. I broke out my collection of cookbooks and made different menus for dinner, started reading my bucket list of books, did an intense "Dutch clean" with sanitizer on every inch of the house like a mad woman, rolled out my yoga mat and tried to master the crow pose, I started purging clothes and old papers and I took to writing. I always wanted to blog, so I found word press and got started with my blog name of flamingo flocks and thoughts. I also used social media as an outlet during lock down and started posting about you guessed it, coffee mugs. My brother gave me advice to write about something familiar to me. Well, I know coffee and I love my mugs, why not?

What I found in my daily coffee mug posts was a little surprising to me. I'm sure several social media followers thought I lost my mind and gone half-crazy writing about cups. As luck would have it, I did experience good vibes, positive feedback and rays of sunshine.

A friend reached out from across the miles and sent me a LIFE IS GOOD... OUTLOOK MOSTLY SUNNY mug. I love the surf shack feel to the cup and the message that is inscribed. It gave me hope at the time and a reminder that life really is good and that the sun always seems to find a way to shine. As I dug deeper into the box to find who the source of this dose of ceramic vitamin D was radiating from, I found a note that read, "Keep on writing Kitty, keep on creating, keep on spreading your love."

I had to break the "no talking house rules" and find Rustin to tell him about my package that was delivered and to also take a minute to reflect and look at the bigger picture of what I'm to learn and gain from this act of kindness.

My friend and this gifted gesture taught me to applaud someone's dreams and creativity. Encourage others to reach for the stars and in this case the sun. Inspire one another to be the best they can possibly be no matter what the idea or goal is. Even if it's penning about coffee mugs for gracious sakes. Allow everyone to live their best lives and express their feelings and help them find their pot of gold at the end of the rainbow. And above all else, let someone know you believe in them and help them to feel it so much that they believe in themselves and that dreams really do come true. One step, one word, one gesture, one thought, one mug at a time.

The world deserves to be filled with sunshine, surfers, surfboards, woody wagons and sandy beaches. Surfs up and the outlook is mostly sunny.

The Courtesy of Using a Name by

M. Wayne

This coffee thought and memory takes me back to the 1970's. What a decade. I loved the simplicity of life back then; catching lightning bugs, spatting with my brother, Loves Baby Soft perfume, Bonnie Bell Lip Smackers, 45 and 33 vinyl records particularly Shaun Cassidy and his best hit, Da Doo Ron Ron, riding my bike to the pool for swim team practice with my beach towel around my neck, jumping rope, hide and go seek, kick ball, playing outside until it was too dark to see, or until I pushed my luck and that was often, when I would hear the warning of the dinner bell ring and I knew to get home pronto. I so love recalling the fun and mischief and childhood.

One rainy summer day my mother asked me If I wanted to accompany her to the shoppes that were located on Main Street in Butler. At that time, the small Western PA town was thriving and filled with several lovely stores and restaurants, so I was already heading to the front seat of the car yelling shotgun just in case my brother was invited. I also knew that the Hot Dog Shop would make the itinerary for lunch, so I was all in!

Just Mom and I pulled out of the driveway and our first stop was The Unicorn. It was a neat small-town shop that had clever items for sale along with cards and gift wraps. While browsing the aisles of the place filled with all kinds of treats, sweets, tidbits and delectables, I spied a coffee mug that had cats all over it and my name going around the rim and l instantly took a liking to it. I must've been on my best behavior that day because when I presented my mother with my find in the store, to ask if it could go with me, my mom didn't hesitate. I walked out with a gold-crowned HALLMARK bag and a huge smile across my face. I was looking forward to showing my dad my new purchase when we returned home.

My mother and I made it to The Hotdog Shop, and we heard our familiar server shout out to the kitchen grill cooks, "Two hots, pickle also, hold the onions", music to my ears. We enjoyed every bite, hit a few more shoppes then we headed home with my bag in hand, and I was gung-ho to see my father. I should've known a coachable moment was in my near future.

My Dad's name is M Wayne Neal, and I could write a book on MWN life thoughts. The lessons, lectures, sessions, thoughts, whatever's; however, I want to recall them, pretty much happened daily. I may not have liked the communications while they were ushered in but now, I use them often and appreciate them immensely. My Dad was a strict disciplinarian and a school administrator so he managed to bring the principal's office home in many ways and often would present tutorials; my new mug was no exception and used as a learning tool.

While holding and examining my latest prize, My Father said in his very authoritative voice and distinguished tone that was capable of unnerving anyone, "Kitty, isn't it nice to see your name on this mug?" I remember recalling that it certainly was cool to me as I was age six or seven years old at the time and my name was an animal that caused a lot of teasing and harassment for me as a young girl. I also never noticed my name KITTY on knickknacks. "Yes Dad, it is." Where was MWN going with this question?

My dad of course finished his thought process and to this day I try and implement his wisdom on the MWN using names lesson. My father went on to explain and asked me to observe people when you call them by their name. "People will respond to you, and you will find that your conversations will become more engaging when you make them feel important. Using a name makes someone feel significant, noticed and special. Using a forename will allow others to feel more connected with you. Avoid using a pronoun to refer to a person if you know their name if possible."

I made the mistake of calling my father a pronoun one time and one time only. I can still see myself trembling and wishing I could reel my words right back into my mouth when I heard my father say, "Does He have a name?" Yikes! Never again did I address my father using the pronoun HE. My father saw everything and everyone in life with a clear eye, and MW was not going to be addressed below his standards. Rightfully and noted. The etiquette and protocol of my father's thoughts resonate with me to this day.

Going through life, I have noticed and felt the importance of using and hearing a name. I love walking into a familiar bar, restaurant, coffee shop, bakery, boutique, gym, salon etc., and hearing my moniker, "Kitty". There's nothing like becoming the character Norm in the sitcom CHEERS when I walk into someone's home where everybody knows your name and they are always glad you came.

Hearing a name can be like music to someone's ears. We are given them at birth for identity. I'm thankful my dad took the time to identify how important it is to make people feel special, significant and have bonds and connections. I think we all like to be recognized and made to feel like we matter. Could it be as simple as using a name? I'd like to think it is that easy and to have the courtesy to do so and even better to have a special nickname.

Most of the charming stores and The Hot Dog Shop are out of business in the small town of Butler, Pa. I miss those gems from back in the day. And I miss my father's coachable moments tremendously. Thanks M. Wayne Neal for your many life lessons and thoughts, especially the reminder to make sure people feel important, exceptional and noticed. Old School Dad and I like it.

S&H BLINDS & FLOOR... SHOP LOCAL SHOP SMALL and have yourself a ball in a small town.

May of 2018, my mother was going to be turning 90. The nine decades absolutely deserved to be celebrated and I was determined to make it the best evening ever. I love to throw soirees, and this one was going to be my dandiest effort. The night was calling to have all my mother's favorite things. Lamb chops, tenderloin sandwiches with horseradish sauce, sauerkraut balls, crab dip, red wine, scotch of course being served light on the water, a cake that was a resemblance of a scotch barrel, old fashions with lots of candied oranges, flowers everywhere and the music had to be a bag pipe player to bring two of my mothers' favorite countries, Ireland and Scotland to Sandusky Ohio. Everything had been taken care of and the final task to complete was to order balloons. I think balloons have a magic about them and always add to the festivities. I wanted 90 of them in my mom's favorite colors.

A friend of mine that is a "show up and just do it, help me enjoy my journey kind of friend" was already assisting me with a party to do, also offered to go pick up the balloons for me. My bud asked me where I was going to place the balloon order. I thought I would go to the party supply store that was a national chain. I really didn't give it much thought to where I should order the balloons. I was more concerned about a check mark on my party to do list.

In an almost shy, not wanting to impose manner, Ed asked if he could suggest a place. Eddie-O is very insightful, and we often have in-depth conversations on just about anything and everything in life. I was curious about where and what my bud was thinking. Ed went on to explain to me that any time any business could go to a small local shop, it always is nice to give them consideration for the job. No matter the size of the project, consider a small operation if they can do it. Every little bit helps keep the small businesses and small towns going. Not being a business owner, this was certainly great food for thought and point well taken. The party balloons were ordered at a small, local business and my friend once again gave me something to think about.

The conversation we had, sure, was about balloons. However, it became so much more to me. It helped me reflect on what inspired Eddie's suggestion.

Ed began working for a small business owner in 1978 for a company that had been in operation since 1947. My friend and his wife purchased this very same business in 1988, and it is still going strong today. The family-owned business owners raised 4 incredible young men that are respectful and successful in their own ways, and all have wonderful families. My husband and I know this family very well and the morals, values and beliefs that are instilled in all of them are something to be proud of, inspirational and second to none. Honesty, hard work, discipline and love are what makes this local family and shop stand loud and proud.

It does make a difference to take your money to the small dream-filled enterprises that exist and operate in the good Old USA. Carpet, blinds, floors, balloons, cakes, cookies, flowers, food, clothing, whatever the order, take it and keep it local. It puts food on tables and keeps traditions and visions alive. SHOP LOCAL SHOP SMALL and have yourself a ball in a small town.

SOMETIMES I WISH I WAS AN OCTOPUS SO I COULD SLAP EIGHT PEOPLE AT ONCE...KEEP CALM AND SLAP ON...NO JUDGEMENT ZONE.

Oh, come on now, let's be real for a minute, shall we? You may not wish for eight appendages to slap someone after a comment, situation or anything that didn't settle right for you; but a good retort, timely delivery, clever reaction or a one-line self-zinger may just bring a smile to your face when someone doesn't quite react the way you were hoping. I think this scenario happens to all of us at one time or another.

I try to manage my reactions to the actions and keep the slaps to myself. I loathe recalling moments with thoughts of wishing I would've said something ultrasmart or just walked away. I don't always succeed at controlling my emotions with grace, but practice makes perfect and so does having someone to discuss, brainstorm and rehash any life event that may arise and most importantly having a friend that permits a "no judgement zone".

This mug was gifted to me from an extremely real, wise, quick-witted friend that just gets and allows me to be me. We have always had a bond and mutual understanding of each other, share a likeness and common ground on many things but also recognize that sometimes in life either one of us may want to take the gloves off and come out swinging, and we permit each other to do so and then we can carry on in our "Que Sera Sera" fashion.

I think we all need a human sounding board in life. Someone who encourages you to speak your own mind, let out your thoughts and feelings openly and not be judged. I don't necessarily need someone to agree with my thoughts and actions. I truly do appreciate honest, sincere, open-minded feedback and the comfort of knowing that those appendages are coming for a hug after our heart to heart instead of a brush-off. It's such a blessing to have friends that allow us to reach new levels in life instead of taking us back to places we have outgrown and moments we would rather forget. I love being able to talk "stuff" out with someone and we see things and situations from each other's perspectives instead of having the need to be right.

I think we have all tried our hand at stone skipping and maybe hit a glass house along the way. Perhaps I should speak for myself and admit that I am guilty of shattering windowpanes.

I choose to use those fractures as chances to reflect, heal, learn and start with a clean sheet as opposed to playing the victim and running from challenges and personal growth opportunities. I'm never the person to feel scornful and expect others to follow suit with the attitude of "how dare you speak to her; you know what she did to me." That I know for sure is not my mode. I recently had an experience where I had to refine, rectify and make a fresh start. That clean up time for me has helped me become quite adequate at putting into practice that it is really none of my business how others think about and view me. A dear friend of mine always states, "sweep off your own back porch". I'm picking up my old corn straw broom and cleaning away at my day in day out hustle and bustle and clearing the cobwebs.

As I'm running this test of endurance in life, I'm thankful for buds that help me when I fall, nudge me to get back in my lane and cheer me as I cross the finish line with the checkered flag waving. That is when I know I have arms to jump into and feel the love of hugs and know that I have entered the no judgment zone. No place like it.

I think it's important for all of us to remember that no one is perfect, give someone enough rope and allowances and have an understanding that life is going to deal us disappointments even amongst the closest of friends. Kindness is power and I'm beyond grateful for the hugs of forgiveness from friends and family when I come up swinging.

My mother has a way of looking at life and the bumps that can come along with it. I love her thought process of, "this situation is just a chapter, not your life story. Think about what you are to learn, take notes, write about it if it helps to ease your mind and heart, then close the chapter as best you can and move on with your book."

I have written a lot of chapters mom; some are hair-raising and perhaps caused your premature beautiful grey head of hair. I'm going to try and proceed like you do and have a strong sense of right and wrong, move with love, grace, giving it my Pat Benatar shot and do my best to live from my heart and go for eight hugs at a time.

FUNK YEAH- JUST. KEEP. MOVING. – ONE SPLAT POINT AT A TIME even if I don't want to show up

Flight attendants are the most highly visible employees and spend the most time with the customers. Delta seemed to find an exuberant number of ways to remind the cadre numbering over 28,000 of the proven statement of our presence and wanting us to be noticeable and hard at work. We can be found with smiles in the aisles (most times), galleys, jump seats and crew quarters. I'll admit there were many days

I wanted to stay in my single bunk and hide from the chaos and extend my break time. I loved climbing in my bed, snapping the curtain, pulling the cozy blanket over me and just when I'm about to drift away it never failed where I was remembering I forgot to get someone, something. I still managed to slumber as I knew my colleagues had my back.

Crew rests is so important and necessary as we adjust to the extreme time zone changes and quick turns of the planes back to the States. Combine the body clocks of each of us trying to synch up with the sun, along with the pace of the job requirements and feeling the need to be ready for show time and spring into action for just about anything to happen. One thing that is never heard from a flight attendant is how unamused they are during work hours.

Often, the "Ons" for the flight down times are spent engaging in conversations with customers and believe it or not, the one-on-one small talks could be the most challenging. It always seemed to me that I was learning something new every day at work or getting humbled. The discussions could go from extremely riveting topics, to ordinary "how is the weather type of dialogue?". Never once was I bored and felt like I was watching the paint dry. Some of the chatters, I put aside from memory. This coffee thought is not one of them as the notions are very positive and became life changing for me.

I was on what is notoriously known for being the best segment of the trip as it was the last leg/flight home of a 3-day tour, and I was ready to land at my Orlando base. The flight was a long haul from California to Florida and I was chit chatting with a guest in the back galley of a 757 aircraft. Our conversation was about working out and what I did for physical activity. I was thirty-something of age and the gentleman passenger, I'm guessing to be in his 40's, I learned was a personal trainer and inquired about my exercise routine. I proudly went on to explain that my husband and I walk 5-6 miles when our schedules permit since we both travel for work, and we were on average walking approximately four days a week. I thought this was a fabulous answer. The trainer responded with exactly what I didn't want to hear by saying, "You do realize that walking is not enough?". My face, I'm certain looked completely stunned as I was thinking this dude is out of his mind. He then went on to suggest to me to give it and myself time and in a few years, I will find it necessary that I add more challenges to my workout regime. How spot on my ship that passed in the night or in this case afternoon encounter came to be.

It seems that I'm destined for life to enjoy wine and dining. With my hobby of imbibing magnificent juice and my ability to eat like a horse, I noticed as the clock was ticking, that maybe, just maybe my one foot in front of the other sneaker workout wasn't quite enough and my years ago passenger was on to something. I needed to add more to my health routine. A little stretching, more cardio and lord help me, I had to pick up some free weights.

I luckily found great choices that suited me along the way that have helped me to feel better mentally and physically. I still find that vino and eating are central in my life, luckily now my workouts are helping to release endorphins and fuel this aging body with energy and strength. I truly notice a difference in how I feel when I can't get to my studio, yoga hot house or gym.

Another aspect that I enjoy about exercising and which helps pass the time is the music that plays during my sessions. I love the tunes that echo off the walls and if the song I hear reminds me of someone, I take the time to send a positive vibe their way. The beat of the ditty playing helps me shift into changing gears and keeps me focused on working out a little bit harder.

Funky Buddha Yoga Hothouse, Tim Dorsey Fitness and Orange Theory have been my Godsends. These three different workouts have been instrumental in me trying to stay in shape and have been a mental and physical healthy release.

I'm thankful for every intention set, high five, fist pump and splat point that have encouraged me to keep going so that I may reach my greatest physical condition. Taking care of me will always be ongoing, a work in progress. A morning ritual that comes right after my Coffee Life Thoughts one cup at a time of course.

I'm always relieved after a completed workout and feel a sense of accomplishment when I'm walking out the door, perspiring a bit, feeling a tad bit like a BAD ASS.

I believe it is so important to find ways to exert ourselves in physical activities and challenges to get our bodies in motion. There are three words from Tim Dorsey Fitness that have changed my life, and I try to live by Tim's Mantra of JUST.KEEP. MOVING. I have a TDF sweatshirt that reads "SORRY I'M LATE…I DIDN'T WANT TO SHOW UP". That says it in a nutshell, how I feel most days pre-work out. Thank you, Tim, for being a spark plug to so many and a kick in the pants. Long May You Run TD.

JUST.KEEP. MOVING. I promise it will turn your life for the better and you will feel strong, healthy and justified in ordering that second glass of well-deserved wine on your next air travel trip.

I'm glad I crossed paths all those years ago and had such an interesting conversation with the soul-stirring trainer. What a difference and possibly life changing a day and back and forth meeting can make.

WAFFLE HOUSE OPEN 24-7 365 DAYS A YEAR Unlock your heart.

There's a popular myth that Waffle House restaurants don't have locks on their doors because they're open 24/7, 365 days a year. I can personally attest to their round-the-clock service. One Christmas, during a layover with Delta Airlines in Cincinnati, Ohio, my parents joined me for dinner. The only restaurant we found open was Waffle House. We enjoyed a holiday feast of eggs, bacon, grits, waffles, butter, and plenty of syrup—a simple yet delicious meal. I'll always cherish that memory, grateful for the warmth of my parents' company and their effort to travel the distance just to be with me.

Waffle House has come to have quite a presence in my life. The batter turned crisp tire tread like treat is one of my sons' favorite meals. Jon Ross other than steak, snow crab legs or a big juicy porkchop, could eat waffles for every meal. If I ask JR after he travels somewhere, I know that this chain restaurant made the itinerary during his trips. I also know that it was a staple visit during his college years. Every time I drive by a Waffle House restaurant anywhere, my thoughts immediately go to J.R.

I met Jon Ross when he was five years old. The cutest little boy with big brown eyes that were filled with magic and mischief. How right I was when my first introduction to Jon Ross resulted in his bouncing a golf ball in his grandmother's kitchen off the floor to the dishwasher causing a huge forever dent on the door, just missing the windows. The reaction from JR's father was one I will never forget. I was smitten and intrigued with them both. The three of us have now formed a family and have been on an adventure ever since. The challenges that we have tackled together have made us strong and resilient. So much so that I don't think there is anything that we can't take on together and conquer. Nothing can stop us, and we will always prevail. Our life together hasn't always been a bed of roses and luckily for us, Rustin allowed Jon Ross and I to put on the boxing gloves, enter the ring, duke out our battles and learn to open and unlock our hearts to each other and both of us winning the round.

Of all the people in the world, the one and only person, Jon Ross, has saved my soul and made my biggest dream come true. All I ever really wanted in life was to be a mom. Jon Ross gives me that opportunity in his way every day and that and he are my biggest blessings. I'm the lucky one. I'm grateful that I've unlocked my heart, 24-7, 365 days a year to an incredible young man and of course to waffles, many, many waffles. Oh, and yes, this mug was a gift from JR, and it is my favorite.

The Ups and Downs of Being a Fan... GIVE IT UP FOR

KC & The Sunshine Band

Rustin and I were heading out for the evening in Roanoke, Virginia and bumped into our neighbor who was curious about what was on our docket for the weekend. I instantly broke out singing the lyrics of GIVE IT UP by KC & The Sunshine Band so that our neighbor could guess that we were on our way to hear my guy KC. My

70's crush was in town, and I wanted to be front and center for the concert. The three of us went on to name several of the band's titles and we kept coming up with hit after hit. Our neighbor said something that struck me in that conversation that I absolutely loved. Ed made the comment about how important it is to be a FAN; it doesn't matter what kind of FAN but to have a love, passion, curiosity for a team, band, sport, something to be Fanatic about. People can be complete strangers but if you know you share the bond of being fans of the same teams, musicians, dignitaries, anything or anyone that has a fan base can bring instant camaraderie. It makes life more fun when we share bonds and connections. What true thoughts and statements.

We went to see KC that evening, along with a thousand give or take of the band's fans that were singing, dancing and having a ball. I kept recalling what my neighbor said earlier about bonding and connecting as I observed the attendees reciting the lyrics and knowing all of them as the Solid Gold dance moves were happening and we were getting our "Get Down Tonight"ing on with KC and his band.

For 17 years, my husband, Jon Ross and I lived in Sandusky Ohio, and we were three out of five Steeler fans that lived in the town on the shores of Lake Erie. To us the best days of the year when we lived in Sandtown were the match up meetings with our Pittsburgh Steelers going head-to head with the Cleveland Browns.

The bantering starts early in the morning with my husband's phone pinging away about the afternoon or evening duel. Rustin is somewhat of an antagonist when it comes to sports, so he loves smack talking and starts it most of the time. He seems to find a string of insults with Browns, Bengals, Cowboys or as Rustin refers to as Cowgirls, Penn State, Michigan, Michigan State… any fans that are the opponents of the Steelers, Ohio State and The Pitt Panthers. We laugh at the retorts coming through and it makes life fun to be a fan. We are proud of our Pittsburgh roots and love the fact that our son graduated from THE Ohio State University and is a huge Buckeye fan. Rustin, Jon Ross and my father are all graduates of the University of Pittsburgh, so we also have a passion for The Pitt Panthers. We live for football season and love the connections that keep us together with our friends ACROSS THE MILES.

There's so much in life that can make us fans. I often find myself using the term, I'M A FAN or stating BIG FAN when I find something that makes me feel happy or piques my curiosity. I like coffee, food, wine, music, restaurants, clothes, books, football, cooking, yoga, movies, dogs, exercise, golf, interior design, Frida Kahlo, Georgia

O'Keefe and my favorite podcast motivational speaker Mel Robbins. All these past times and people help to make me feel fanatical. It feels good to have interests and hobbies and with those often brings connections and bonds. Sometimes the loop can be with just myself and that is always a good reboot for the soul.

My neighbor said, "I love it when people are fans, and they are good at it." I love that as well. It makes life so much fun to cheer and root for teams, people, and things that help us to feel alive. I love having past times that forever link me to some of my favorite people on earth.

Bring on football season. You can bet we will be at Gar's Bar or Thirsty Pony physically in our YINZER gear or by phone cheering on our Steel City, loving life and our friends with the ups and downs of being a FAN. And GIVE IT UP for KC & The SUNSHINE BAND. BIG FAN!

PICTURE IT SICILY 1922...THE GOLDEN GIRLS... Thank you for being a friend of all ages.

BIG FAN of THE GOLDEN GIRLS! This sitcom has special memories for me as I remember watching this with my parents in our family room quite often and my dad chuckling at the one-line zingers delivered by the matriarch Sophia, headstrong

Dorothy, Southern belle Blan-che and sweet but bewildered Rose. The series is based on four older single women living together sharing a home in Miami Florida. Three happen to be widows and one is a divorcee. The writers of this show to me are the best in the business. The lines that the Girls deliver are priceless, and I still laugh every time no matter how many repeats I have viewed.

I love how these women have formed bonds with each other, and they all seem to look to the eldest Sophia, for wisdom, strength, humor and love as she shares her life thoughts often kicking off with the words 'PICTURE IT SICILY 1922". The three younger roommates anxiously wait for Sophia to deliver her message, and her words have a moral to the story and the roommates seem to grow, laugh and learn. Sometimes the tale results in Sophia's daughter Dorothy stating, "Shady Pines Ma, Shady Pines". That statement is a threat to send Sophia back to the nursing home if she doesn't behave. However, most of the time, the framed story is a life lesson for the roommates and Sophia's thoughts, seem to give these Golden Friends something to think about and definition helping them to find comfort and solutions in their time together that always seems to conclude with the friends celebrating their life thoughts and victories sharing cheesecake.

This show not only has me wondering who my three roommates in Miami would be in my sunset years, but it has always made me appreciate the importance of having friends of all ages.

I feel fortunate to have friends that range from 18-98 years of age. I love to learn and take in the experiences that come with the different age brackets. Hanging out with a much younger generation can bring a new, fresh outlook on life. Technology for one is something I need a lot of assistance with and tutoring. Our young friends arrive and within minutes I can feel like the latest and greatest techie after they take the time to install for me the new-fangled apps and gadgets along with very patient tutorials so I'm not feeling lost when they leave me to operate my new programs solo.

I also love the energy of young people. We (Rustin and I) sit back in awe and watch the laughter and the detailed descriptions from the events that happened the night before. We always find it astonishing that they are up and still standing. I'm impressed and thankful they are breathing and ready to go back in action and make some more bad decisions. Our sons' friends and our compadres children have become our companions now that they are adults, and it is so refreshing, and time well invested. We brunch, have house visitors, pub hop, coffee, wine, dine, enjoy cigars, attend sporting events; we do all kinds of activities with a group from the younger generation, and it is always full of fun, laughs and memories. The immersion of our worlds helps to keep us young.

I will always love to soak up the sun and energy and hang out with our younger chums, however, I can't forget about the golden oldies. Golden Girls, Golden Boys, doesn't matter, bring them on because there is a plethora of wisdom and information to learn from the elder generation.

I fondly recall sitting in a local well known watering hole on Kelley's Island, Ohio, and listening to my bud's father tell me about his recollection of WW II that was experienced firsthand. I felt like I was there in action and paid attention to every detail of our conversation to get my own personal history lesson. I listened to Papa K tell me about the most destructive conflict in human history and his personal story with that sparkle and a tear in his eye.

That very same day, in The Village Pump, I hopped over to a different barstool and engaged with another one of my friend's fathers that was 90 at the time and known as the best of the best on Lake Erie for sailing. I listened to the natural storyteller go in depth about the history of Kelley's Island and the shenanigans that transpired on what used to be called Island Number 6. FASCINATING. Lee Brown never stated my husband's name correctly. Rustin became Thurston, Dustin, Justin. I recall only once that Mr. Brown called Rustin by his given name. I like to believe that LB's misnaming was intentional, just for amusement and to stir things up a bit. It did bring smiles to so many, including Dustin.

I recall my grandmother so adoringly and remember learning so many tidbits about how to keep a house, work in the kitchen, garden and how to gather family and friends around a table or in your home, especially with homemade noodles and chicken dinner. I observed how my grandmother made sure the pennies were piling up in the piggy bank and stretching a dollar bill whenever possible because of living and surviving the Depression. That piling and stretching has rubbed off on my mother and has served her well. I'm working on my own version of penny-pinching. I'm not the best pincher but I'm giving it my best pinch.

I have a 96-year-old Aunt who is a master at coin-pinching (except when it comes to buying jewelry), that I wouldn't trade for all the money in the world. We travel and lunch, talk and strategize our Steelers and we go shopping. I find myself getting very annoyed when I'm driving on our girl's day out since my Aunt Goldie feels it is her duty to turn into a portable crossing guard and point out to me every stop sign and traffic signal along the way. I also know that I will miss the suggestions very much someday.

My mother-in-law Norma had such a strong work ethic and was so talented, creative and used her hands to bring into being anything we desired. Window treatments, Steeler wine bottle wraps, baking, sewing, mending any garment that would need altered, homemade pretzels that her grandson is marketing now calling the crispy baked treats… GRAMS PRETZELS, waffles, funnel cakes; the list could continue. Norma did so much but was the best at loving her family. I loved to watch her face glow when all her sons were home and together.

My father-in-law reminded me fondly of Walter Matthau's character in Grumpy Old Men. Richard could be curmudgeonly, however I found him charming and challenging. I was referred to as the Old Ball and Chain, but I also knew I had him wrapped around my little pinky. Richard was extremely intelligent and did every task to the nines. No exceptions. I always enjoyed my conversations with him. I laughed and my spirits were lifted after our time together. Each time I walked away learning something from The Old Putz; that nickname was turnabout fair play, fitting and fun for my humorous "Dad". I miss our bantering and him very much.

I grew up watching my parents nurture friendships ACROSS THE MILES for years with friends that they had to leave behind due to geographical moves but kept in touch and to this day, my mother still has the friendships intact, and they have become a part of my life. In fact, I attribute my love of coffee mugs to my Aunt Wanda who is a friend that has been in my life for 50 plus years and makes the world's best sweet tea and has the sweetest heart to match. My Uncle Bun that belongs to Wanda has taught me the art of listening and conversation, the importance of sport coat traditions and how to make the world's best craft cocktails. True Classics.

I have several friends that are close to twenty years my senior and have a bona fide edge on daily and life happenings that helps me see people and things in a different light and offers a fresh perspective. Growing and learning with my wise older friends if you will has helped me to become balanced, humble and the best first-rate version of myself. I'm concluding that as we age, we become more authentic and our true selves. I'm enjoying these manifestations with my friends and mostly with me.

I think we learn from everyone and every interaction that we encounter. I truly step back, listen and observe from all walks of life, young and old. What is the familiar saying? Make new friends but keep the old, one is silver and the other gold. I would like to add to that, that of all ages.

Friends from all generations will help us learn, grow, blossom and bloom. Fresh perspectives, energy and wisdom keep us feeling alive, living in the moment and curious about what makes the world spin and people tick. Mentors and partners in crime can be of any age. Look for inspiration and input from all; especially the Sophias of the world.

Watch, listen and learn from each other. A variety of ages of friends and acquaintances may cause your life to come full circle with an abundance of love and well roundedness that we never thought imaginable. The learning and growth possibilities seem endless to me.

May we always have the spunk and spark in us so that we hear the threat of "Shady Pines Ma, Shady Pines", after a little bit of mischief at any age. Here's to us being young at heart. Thank you for being a Friend, of all ages. Now who wants cheesecake?

Butterflies are free to fly...look for the signs.

Butterflies have a way of captivating, enchanting and charming me; they always bring a smile to my face. The delicate, whimsical, winged beauties to me symbolize hope, strength, comfort, positivity and grace. This mug and the artwork on it came from the heart of a special young lady at a time when I needed all the above positive vibes as possible. I was knee deep or perhaps more like neck deep in grief after my father passed and was struggling at times to catch my breath.

A friend and I at that time when I was detached and overwhelmingly sad met daily for morning walks at a beautiful area in Ohio called Sheldon Marsh State Nature Preserve Beach. This treasure that has a walking trail that leads to the Lake Erie Shorelines is also known as one of Ohio's premier birding locations with over 300+species and wildflowers. This gem that was our AM paradise also was loaded with butterflies that followed us daily the entire walk. My sweet friend that was desperate to say anything to make me smile pointed out the consistent butterflies that joined us day-to-day and told me that they were there for us as a sign that my father was just fine, more than fine but wanted me to be just fine as well and MW was checking in on us. Without a doubt the brilliant, colorful species didn't miss a minute of our exercise routine, tagging along from the parking lot to the beach area. They were great walking partners as we got our groove on, and my angel on earth listened to my daily emptiness, sometimes not needing to say a word, just there for me, trying to get me out of my funk. And when I tell you those butterflies were there daily, they were and not just one, at least 10 every morning flew behind or beside us the entire journey.

I began to look for butterflies to give me a sign that all was going to be alright, and life can transform for me, and I will find my own wings again to continue with strength. Grief never really does go away but luckily for me; I had friends and family that helped me look for signs to carry on and manage it. Signs are everywhere, and it's fun to look for and use them as guidance.

Shortly after my father's passing, my brother and I were concerned about my mom. Starting life over after 55 years of marriage and having to reinvent herself and her life, caused us both to worry about what was next for our mother. We also thought that perhaps mom was losing it a bit because we kept hearing about this cardinal that kept visiting and wouldn't leave. The bright red bird from my understanding was racing from window to window at my mom's and tapped all day long seeming to want into the house. I thought to myself, how much can my mom's new friend be around? I decided to go visit for a firsthand look. Low and behold, this bird was casing the joint and was there 24-7; my mother was not losing mind. The tapping and flying around was constant and comical. We weren't quite sure what to do with our new pet that was not leaving. My brother came home from Florida for a visit and was intrigued with the mischief of our new feather friend and thought he should have a name. Jeff named our guest Gibson, after Bob Gibson a well-known St. Louis Cardinal. Gibson, stayed for quite some time and we learned that cardinals appear when angels are near and that they represent loved ones that passed away. I'll take that thought and relish in the comfort of hope. Cardinals are also thought to mean that you are being blessed with good luck and fortune. Now every time I see a Gibson, I think of my heavenly angels and cherish my sign.

I'm always looking for signs to help me make decisions, complete thoughts and problems. I feel and I'm very aware of the synchronicities that are out there and may appear in many ways and often offer solutions. I have found signals from songs, comments, billboards, coincidences, sayings, dreams, reoccurring dreams, patterns of numbers, gut feelings, Randal El's coffee mugs, license plates; so many ways to make connections and gain a renewed confidence about something or someone through the many signs that can give me what I feel from butterflies: hope, strength, comfort, positivity and grace. My husband and I chose to move to Roanoke Virginia due to the sign, literally a Dr. Pepper billboard that shines brightly at night in the downtown area. Rustin's coffee mugs every morning are a burgundy and white can of his favorite soda and we took the advertisement as our signal to make the move a block away from the lighted bottle cap.

To me it makes life interesting to observe the surroundings of nature and everyday life and the universe. My friend and I laugh about an experience that happened to us as we were told, "I'm just going to let the universe take the wheel and see what happens". We use that saying all the time now. We had no choice but to let the universe take over in our situation and let fate step in. Things worked out just the way we both hoped, as the wheel spun in our favor.

A dear friend recently sent me a quote card that reads "Just when the caterpillar thought the world was over, it became a butterfly". It is my hope that we always look and find signs to keep us smiling, bring joyful tears to our eyes to carry on and delight in the synchronicities along the way.

I so admire you Mom, for taking a giant leap into living an independent life after your life love passed. You consistently have me wondering: How did you get to be who you are? You are resilient, poised, unpretentious, genuine, standing strong and a force of upstandingness in a class all your own. Thank you for teaching me and showing me signs and messages along the way as you started your second life; and of course, for the bright red birds with black masks around their eyes… Gibsons.

THE BIG D. Find A WAY TO GET PAID FOR WHAT YOU LOVE!

I feel many flight attendants have the same story about our flying careers. Often, it seems to be common that most stews/stewards were only going to fly for a year and then move on from the friendly skies. That at least was my plan, that didn't quite work out for me. I retired after 29 years, 11 months and 18 days with Delta Air Lines. Delta keeps track of every second, so I know the exact amount of time I logged with my company. The good, bad and the ugly moments of my flight time come with life thoughts, lessons, notions and lots of motion along with stories to last an eternity right down to the final last walk up the jetway.

My office had windows, wings, engines and seats filled with a cast of characters. It was quite an experience to report to work on a Big Old Jet Airliner and soar around the world never knowing what each day would bring. I learned something new every day whether it be a fun interesting fact, how to deal with all walks of life and the Irish Diplomacy of, "The art of telling someone to go to hell and having them look forward to the trip". I do love the Irish, I'm one of them and I'm married to one of them, it's in "me" blood.

The friendships that are made with fellow crew members are what I refer to as our own Sorority/ Fraternity in the sky. We ourselves come from all over the world, have different upbringings, languages and views on life. However, when push comes to shove, we are there for each other as a team and have each other's backs and are trained to do so. We don't mess around when it comes to safety, standing by each other and working together for positive end results. The fun and bonds of flight attendant friendships are second to none. We are a group of individuals that travel all over the Globe together, never knowing what can be around the corner. We depend on each other for support, help, smiles, laughs and tears and maybe just maybe that one more quiet glass of wine.

I didn't always love my job, in fact, I have an Orlando based supervisor and two very dear friends that counseled me several times to stick it out, do not make any harsh decisions and realize the golden nugget that could be lost. You never really know what someone is going through in life and I'm grateful that I had support and listening ears to help me come to the resolution to keep on flying.

I'm humbled and honored that I got to work for such a wonderful company and meet so many millions of people. I'm even more pleased that I have lifetime friends that are with me in my heart always. I'm so thankful I got paid to see the world and have love, memories and scars to prove it. I feel blessed for every lesson, life thought and growing experience that helped me to become the person I am today. I'm beyond grateful my parents waved all those years ago as I boarded the plane to start a new life, career and opportunity that saved me in many ways.

Find something you love to do and get paid for it. Thanks Delta and the world's best colleagues and friends and for a million memories. I'm honored to have worked with the best of the best one sky mile at a time.

The Life Bucket Lists for Cans of Chock-full o' nuts.

I was home on one of the ACROSS THE MILES visits with my parents and we decided to be a little old-fashioned and went to see a movie in the local theater instead of watching the latest on Netflix. I loved going to catch a show with my father as it always entailed a trip to the refreshment stand. Popcorn with extra salt and butter, Whoppers, Milk Duds and beverages were being balanced in our hands as we made the way to our seats.

We decided to see my favorite actor, Jack Nicholson in his latest great "The Bucket List". This movie night out is sentimental for me and top of my list for several reasons. First, on my why's this night holds a place in my heart is that my crystal ball was out of commission so I had no way of knowing at the time that our evening out would be my father's final trip to get his favorite snacks and enjoy a movie. That night my father made a second trip to refill his jumbo container of the puffed corn kernels, soda and came back with a fresh box of junior mints. M Wayne made snacks and mealtimes so fun because he loved to eat any type of food, was great at it and made no bones about it. Secondly, I love the song SAY by John Mayer that is played at the end of the movie. The lyrics encourage us to love, open our hearts and say what we need to say to our loved ones. The timing was perfect for me considering this was my last trip to the cinema with my favorite epicurean. Finally, the plot and characters of the movie is and are very interesting, ever so comical and extremely inspirational.

The storyline of the movie includes a billionaire and an auto mechanic that are both terminally ill and wind up in the same hospital room. Carter and Edward (characters names in the movie) have personal family situations in their lives that they wish could be different. They also realize time is winding down for them and they have things and places that they both would like to do and see. These two new friends borrow a yellow writing tablet to create a list and vow to start checking off the items together that they have added to and named the bucket list. The list is filled with accomplishments the now more than acquaintances would like to complete before they both kick the bucket so to speak and their ashes are buried in their individual Chock-full o' Nuts coffee cans. Hilarious, thought provoking, tear jerk movie that required for me a purse pack of tissues.

On the ride home with my parents, we were rehashing the movie, and I was already rattling off all the destinations that I planned on adding to my travel spots that I'm now renaming with my catchy new title, The Bucket List. I noticed my father was a little quiet and I inquired as to why the silence. My Dad stated that he was very enthused by my adventurous plans and encouraged me to keep on seeing and learning about our world and to make sure my travel plans on my bucket list included first and foremost visits to Renfrew, PA, my hometown.

However, my father's silence was brought on more due to the reasoning that he didn't want me to forget the everyday details and things to do and accomplish in our lives. Things on a smaller scale. The suggestion was to have many bucket lists that didn't need to include Hot Air Ballooning in Cappadocia, Turkey but perhaps thinking of things to broaden the mind and me and my life skills has a person. Sometimes MWN Life Lessons could be such a buzz kill but I knew my father was on to something and I started thinking about the endless possibilities of bucket lists for me. I found my challenge from my father to be thought provoking.

My dad often would say to me after being somewhere or doing something, "Kitty, always leave an area you visited improved." I thought that my father's almost daily repeated request or suggestion would be a good everyday bucket list to ponder. How many times do we exit a room, kitchen, bathroom, gym, couches with blankets, stores trying on clothes; any place where we spend our days for just a few minutes or maybe hours that may need a little pick up, spruce, courtesy wipe of the sink or some sunshine.? It's nice to show respect and clean up and end on a positive note wherever our travels may take us.

I also keep a running bucket list of interests that are doable by walking or a ground mode of transportation that I try to check the box daily, when possible, especially if I'm exploring an unfamiliar territory. Doing something new and different each day like exploring coffee houses, restaurants, small taverns, gift shops, clothing boutiques, roadside stands, taco trucks, diners, wine bars, theater performances, movies, comedy acts, art galleries, museums, bookstores are all examples of smaller scaled down bucket lists goals. I'm constantly adding to this one, and I love the possibilities of the day-to-day adventures. This list always keeps me looking for fresh ideas to seek and experience.

Of course, there is my Big Bucket List of Travel. This list seems to make my husband a little nervous. It is an ongoing lengthy list of ideas and dreams that I love to think about how I'm going to do it all and when. Life has stepped in a bit, and I need to take a little hiatus from the biggie list. I am thankful for each completed wish I have already checked and will get to it when it seems appropriate for me to do so. Sometimes you must do what you must do.

The Health and Wellness yellow tablet page must be a daily check for me. This list is not optional with my love of groceries that I inherited from my father. I do something every day to keep myself in motion and look forward to adding new ways to move and groove. I'm fortunate that I have some life thoughts and mentors that motivate me to get to my workouts or this list would be a struggle. I always feel accomplished when I make that daily health and wellness check mark.

My favorite bucket list is one that I refer to as the Pay it Forward Bucket List. I simply love the concept of Paying it Forward. I will never forget when someone does something for me to make my life or a loved one's a little bit easier, comfortable, leaving a smile on faces. That to me is what life is and should be all about. I like to try and do something that makes me laugh and bring joyful tears to my eyes every day. One thing that is always a constant and a guarantee that I have found, is when you do for others, pay the kindness forward, you will have joyful tears in your eyes and your soul will be belly laughing with gusto. That feeling, you can't beat with a stick and is worth all the check marks in this big, beautiful world on our bucket lists.

Get out there and say what you need to say, check mark those bucket lists of ideas on your yellow writing tablets so your own personal can of Chock-full o' Nuts will be completely full, with a smile on your heart knowing you lived your best life to the fullest and made people smile and live a little bit easier because of you and your kindness... along the way.

Breaking Waves at THE BREAKERS … JUST KYLE IT.

My brother moved to Lake Worth, Florida now called Lake Worth Beach, in the summer of 1985. I was getting ready to start my freshman year in college that fall. We as a family traveled to the sunshine state to assist and help my one and only sibling get settled and acquainted with his new digs. I loved the atmosphere and scene where he was going to be living and pictured myself with high hopes that this would be my spring break destination for the next four years. Jeff has always managed to make friends easily and luckily for me, one of my brother's new buds knew the area well and offered to take my family on a tour of the hot spots of the area. Did I mention this friend was blonde, looked like he stepped right off the beach from Malibu California and had the best personality to match his JAMZ surfer shorts? Sign me up for what I'm hoping to be an all-day tour.

Kyle, our tour guide shows up at my bros in an outfit that did not disappoint. Surfer shorts, a ripped sleeveless t-shirt and flip flops. We climbed into my parents' car, and I managed to get the perfect seat right next to the surfer. Having never been to Lake Worth, I instantly fell in love with the area in which the motto is "Where the Tropics Begin'. Very cool vibes come from the eclectic downtown area filled with specialty shops, art galleries, historic buildings, bars and restaurants. Lake Worth is about 60 miles North of Miami and just south of West Palm Beach. Very charming and laid-back beach town as walking, driving, cycling and skateboarding to the beach over the draw bridge is what the locals do.

Our tour continues after a quick snack at a local deli in downtown LW and we are heading North on A1A on what I still consider to this day, one of my favorite drives. Mansion after mansion with the beautiful, manicured lawns and the exquisite turquoise color of the Atlantic Ocean splashing into the private sandy beaches is just so magnificent. We ended up in Ritzy West Palm and I'm instantly intrigued. I fell in love with the perfectly lined palm tree streets, architecture of the buildings and the cleanliness of the chic coastal town. We found the well-known Worth Avenue and strolled the street and admired the shops and restaurants. I loved watching the pampered pooches sip water from the beautiful, imported pottery bowls on the Avenue. Kyle wondered if we were thirsty like the pooches seemed to be and asked if we would like to imbibe in an afternoon cocktail. I wasn't the legal drinking age at the time, but iced tea always works for me, so we made our way to the most amazing Seaside Glamour place, THE BREAKERS. To this day, one of my favorite things to look for in my travels is the oldest hotel in every city I visit that is in existence, find the bar and treat myself to their house specialty. Perhaps this tour from long ago inspired my past time. I was captivated by this Grand Old Beauty that was established in 1896.

We were making our way through the luxury resort when suddenly, our gorgeous guide is stopped by a very distinguished man dressed in black tie. The gentleman that was employed by THE BREAKERS ever so gently taps Kyle on the shoulder and proceeds to explain the dress code for the Breakers that Kyle was obviously not following. The well-mannered employee kindly asked our tour guide if he would please remove himself from the premises. My surfer in a very respectful, articulate manner and without delay, responds with this clever retort, "I would like to thank you, because of you and The Breakers I will always be able to say, that I have been kicked out of better establishments when I'm dismissed again." Kyle turned to us and said, "Ready to go family"? Without missing a beat and none of us really knowing what to do, we filed out of the Breakers and continued with our day. To my amazement, Kyle could've cared less, never mentioned it or was phased by the situation. Rules are rules and meant to be followed, it wasn't personal to my favorite tour guide and was insignificant in his big picture. I loved how the situation was handled.

Often on the aisles of the airplane, situations would frequently seem to come about, and as I was doing my daily mental self-talk on how to handle my new fresh hell, I often thought of my blonde surfer and decided to "Kyle It" with ease of confidence and ever so nonchalant. Kyle was my first introduction to "Don't Sweat the Small Stuff" and I loved it. Humor, wit, tenacity and grit kept our family tour in motion that day and I put into service those traits to carry on during my long, often challenging workdays.

The memorable outing back in 1985 ended with a fantastic stop for dinner at a local Cuban restaurant. I tried Ropa Viejas that evening and sweet plantains. My first experience with Cuban food and I'm forever hooked. Kyle explained to me that my dish translation means "old clothes". I thought my food selection was appropriate to order since my tour guide was dressed in his favorite old duds.

I have returned to the luxury resort in Palm Beach and was very conscientious not to wear my ripped jeans that are usually my staple go to favorite. I think back fondly to that day, my family and of course the surfer that taught me to try to roll with the punches and keep on keeping on.

Thank you, Kyle, for the Surfs Up attitude and a fun memory for my family. May I always remember to just "KYLE IT"! I also gained Kyles line to add and use to my repertoire just in case I was dismissed from a Bistro in Napa Valley for not using my indoor voice when my Steelers were playing in the Super Bowl. I told you I was a Big Fan. 😊

Benny's on the Beach... time to soak up and spread the sunshine

I've been patronizing Benny's since the year it opened in 1986. Every visit to my brothers, I manage to make it to the fishing pier on Lake Worth Beach and pop into my favorite bar/restaurant that is perched right on the Atlantic Ocean. The food is outstanding, and I love the surfside dining and the vibe of this place. The Seafood bake, Spanish paella on the weekends and the eggs benedict are always a hit with me. I usually sit at the bar after a walk on the beach, order a Sauvignon Blanc and take in the scene as the bartenders and staff hustle to keep everyone happy. The restaurant's motto is "Where Every Day is a Vacation". They certainly own that statement as that is what it feels like to me at Benny's, VACATION.

One afternoon after a stroll on the beach, I made my way to my favorite outside spot, ordered wine and iced tea and peeked at the menu. As I was seated, I noticed this very eccentric looking woman I would guess to be in her sixties. She was dressed to the nines and had the cutest little punt pass and kick dog. That is my husband's and his buddy's term for a small pooch. Not sure of the breed but the dog was in a shirt and pants, sitting there looking very aloof and human. I had to comment on the dog's vibe. The owner who reminded me of the outlandish blonde Katherine, in the movie UNDER THE TUSCAN SUN, was very appreciative of my compliment, and we started to engage in small talk. I learned through our chit chatting that the dog's name was Buster. I had a Buster in my life once and that one still has my heart. A cinnamon-colored Chow that Rustin loved to call "Lawsuit" or "Alligator with fur" was my top dog and I miss my lion look-like companion immensely.

It turns out that my new acquaintance and Buster frequent Benny's and live close by. I learned a little bit of local gossip and some interesting facts about Lake Worth Beach. As we were winding down our conversation, my fast friend made the statement that she was off to find and spread the sunshine. It was a beautiful day at the beach and the sun was shining ever so brightly. I commented as I was listening to the Wave Haven that was in my current back yard, "you won't need to go far, a few steps and you have Oceanside Serenity." The local agreed but went on to explain to me her thought process was more than just being in the sun but making the sun…shine. I wasn't quite sure where this conversation was going at the time, but she had my attention. "Katherine" has a daily personal requirement to make or do a kind gesture every day to see a smile on someone's face and hope that they live a little bit easier because of something she did, and she encouraged me to think about adding sunshine and rays to someone during my day.

As my intriguing character gathers her purse, hat and leash for Buster, we bid farewell and pleasantries. I certainly had new ideas to ponder after my uplifting morning and thought how my intriguing new acquaintance met her sunshine quota for the day with me.

I've returned to Benny's several times since my encounter with Miss Sunshine and Buster. I still watch out for them on every visit. Unfortunately, no luck for me. I like to imagine they are in Tuscany, enjoying life and causing a scene at a fountain in a Piazza with all the locals.

I recall fondly my memory at Benny's with my new friend and the compelling way she lives her life. It's a fantastic way to approach each day and each other. Perhaps my chance encounter with "Katherine" and Buster has kept the spark alive for my pay it forward bucket list that I try and incorporate into each day.

I'm grateful for this meet-up with such an interesting woman. I admire her passion for life, doing what is just and being good to others. It's such a fabulous way to tackle each day. I acquired so much from this stranger and I'm beyond grateful for our brief time spent that beautiful sunny morning. Because of this meeting I have been challenged to try every day, to Soak up and SPREAD THE SUNSHINE. I can't think of a better way to exist.

GLORY DAYS AT CLARION UNIVERSITY - BECHT HALL, Greek Life, 537 Madison Street Girls and FINDING BALANCE.

It was early August 1985, and I had a wonderful opportunity to visit with my aunts, one week before I was to start my freshman year at Clarion University of Pennsylvania in Clarion, PA. I found myself a little on edge for many reasons for the new chapter in my life. The biggies were the random roommate assignment, massive change of leaving home for the first time other than summer camps and sleepovers, the sense of the unknown, having to study, missing my mother's meals, leaving my family and high school buds and my bestie and the worst fear for me was… I was going to miss my dog Brandy, the fine girl.

As we were sitting on My Aunt Goldie's wooden porch swing, with chains keeping it to the ceiling and an extremely colorful quilted patched handsewn cushion that I have sat on a thousand times, my aunts were listening to me rattle on intently and then they offered me advice that was delivered with grace and hard truths that I needed to hear.

My mom's sisters proceeded to express their thoughts and ideas for me to develop an understanding of learning how to manage my academic schedule but also to be able to enjoy and cherish every aspect of my college years. I was told going off to school was going to be one of the hardest moments of my life that I would have to navigate on my own. I'm no longer going to be under my parents' roof however, I would still be on their watch. I needed to have a firm plan to study but also to participate in school activities and find time for fun. Diet and rest would be necessary to help me not feel as though I'm on perpetual overload; I will need to find balance in my life. This was the first time I had ever thought about the word balance other than trying to steady myself and remain upright without a fall. What did my aunts mean by finding balance especially with life? I was about to learn quickly.

I set the goal for myself that I would graduate college in a four-year time frame. That stipulation was very important to me. Before I even stepped on campus, I was going to get that accomplished. In High School, I had decent grades without really studying or applying myself. I was more into mischief and friends and had a ball. I wouldn't trade my High School memories for anything. The word was spelled F-U-N, and we had it 24-7.

I knew if I wanted to complete my number 4 goal in years; studying, library time, cracking books and taking notes was going to have to be in the balance table. I took to my newfound study habits and got off to a good start. My fathers' term of nose to the grindstone really did happen for me in college. I didn't partake in alcohol, never missed one class, and I did make my 4-year goal happen. I had to learn how to balance my academics, a boyfriend, eating well, laundry, living arrangements and a job at the college bookstore. Balancing everyday life in college was going alright but I was really missing out on what I enjoyed most, FUN. I was missing zest in my life, and I needed to find my "Joie de vivre" once again.

I was so petrified of failing and not completing my goal that I felt overwhelmed with the responsibility to study. My daily routine seemed to be only academics; all work and no play. I felt like I was missing the boat on what should be 4 fantastic years of life. I had to learn to relax and give up my day-to-day tug of war game of trying to manage my studying and I needed to start my own play time. Fortunately for me I succeeded with a little help from my friends, and I learned that it's okay to not have to appear unruffled or unflappable. College was teaching me about life, and I was willing to be flexible and open and get my own groove back on.

I started remembering what it felt like to have the flow of a life force and started recalling things that I have always enjoyed. My love of music came back to me and with the help of my extremely fun and intelligent next-door neighbor in my dorm; we started our own business of "The Becht Hall DJ Girls" that we conducted in the warm weather right out of my dormitory window of room 209. We would blast my boom box to the highest volume and the thunderous tunes would echo throughout the campus. We accepted song requests, which wasn't an easy task as this was the cassette era days, however, we were successful more times than not. Our tip jar that someone made for us was a Maxwell House Coffee can with a slit on the lid and a sign taped to the tin that read "Cash Only". I loved our entrepreneurial spirit and of course our tunes. We shared the profits and treated ourselves to nights out at one of our local favorite eateries, The Captain Loomis, Bobs Sub or Colegios Pizza.

The Rec Room on Thursday nights in our all-girl dormitory was the place to be and at times was difficult to get a seat, couch or floor space as we all piled in with our Pjs, robes and hair turban towels on and bowls of popcorn to watch the ever so popular, The Cosby Show. After the comedy sitcom we would talk, gossip, laugh and sometimes fall asleep together until the dreaded "lights out" announcement was made, and we had to return to our rooms.

As luck would have it, a High School friend of mine also became a Clarion classmate. Our former mischievous skills came in handy as we spied milk crates from the local grocery store that we wanted to use for housing books in our rooms and a grocery cart to aid in getting the laundry to our dorm utility room that housed our coin operated machines. I should've charged rent for my wheeled wagon as it was in high demand.

My sophomore year, I explored the campus Greek Life and fell in love with the Green and Gold Jacket sorority whose theme song was from the show CHEERS. The sisters knew all the words to the ditty, and they really did know your name. Sign me up, I want in.

From my sorority I found sisters that became roommates for our first apartment and I'm happy to say that we keep in touch with each other to this day. We learned from the experience of living together off campus; the art of grocery shopping, check book balancing, who's up to cook dinner, dust and vacuum chores, having to take turns with hot water for showers, sharing each other's wardrobes, blessed to have a gifted washer and dryer that we had to learn to switch over our loads of clothes immediately as those machines were always running on over load and in constant use,(at one point we started a sign-up sheet as we were serious about our built in laundry mat), first one home during the weekdays from classes was responsible for having the television on to the channel that hosted our favorite soap opera, The Guiding Light. The daytime drama seemed to take precedence to complete as we worked on many challenges of young girls living under one roof at 537 Madison Street.

We attended Alpha Sigma Tau functions together as well as campus life activities and we grew up together arm and arm, hugged, laughed, cried and wiped away each other's tears through our magical college years.

My Aunts Goldie and Grace were very instrumental at putting me on the path to harmony all those years ago about finding balance in life. A job that needs to happen every day. Life, work, health, fitness, relationships, overall well-being is truly all about balance. I'm also happy to note that I have become very good at remembering to have FUN and keep my exuberance for life strong. I must add that I think my husband does balance with the best of them. Work hard, play hard. Make time for fun.

I absolutely cherished my time and memories at C.U.P. I think the greatest take away from my college years, besides the fact that I have gained wonderful lifetime friendships and sisterhood, and thanks to one of my sisters, I can rattle off all the poisonous snakes that exist in the United States; is that I personally learned how to manage everyday tasks and duties. The key is to keep things in check to not become exhausted physically or mentally while mastering the art of multi-tasking.

I'm grateful for my mom's wise sisters for listening to me and offering advice, wisdom and mostly love. I think back fondly on that day and the ease of life of a front porch swing with a glass of iced tea and wonderful aunts coaching me to be prepared for what was up next on deck for me in life and teaching me a skill that I use every day...LIFE BALANCE.

IT'S NEVER TOO LATE TO REINVENT YOUR WHEEL...MAKE IT A POTTERY WHEEL.

One of the perks of living in downtown Roanoke is the convenience of getting around on foot. I walk out my lobby door, make a turn in any direction, and can find restaurants, retailers, museums, coffee houses, hotels, bars, salons, bakeries, yoga studios, breweries, art galleries, cigar clubs, The Mill Mountain Theater, and, on Saturdays, the Farmers Market, which runs from early spring into the Christmas season.

The vendors start setting up their goods around 7:00 am in front of the Historic Roanoke City Market, which has been operating since 1882. Most Saturdays, I head out early with a cup of coffee, baseball hat on backward, sweatshirt, comfy pants, and sneakers to make my selections. The tables are filled with locally grown produce, plants, eggs, cheese, fresh meats, and baked goods. There's also a Blue Ridge Cider donut stand, where the donuts are made fresh and hot on the premises. Artisans offer handcrafted jewelry, artwork, wood carvings, soaps, Christmas ornaments, note cards, and pottery.

One morning, as I cruised by the pottery vendor, the coffee mugs caught my eye, and I had to stop and check out the unique pieces. The artist, noticing my interest, struck up a conversation with me. She explained how she uses doilies to leave impressions in the clay. Each creation was different, with earthy tones and intricate designs. When I found out they were dishwasher-friendly, I bought two mugs because I couldn't decide on just one.

During our conversation, I learned that the artist's name was Nora. She looked to be in her early 70s and told me she was working on her master's degree at Cornell University's College of Agriculture and Life Sciences during the Woodstock era. Her beliefs and opinions didn't align with what was happening in the world at that time, and feeling the need to escape for a while, she decided to explore her town of Ithaca, New York.

As she wandered in and out of local stores, she stopped at a pottery shop, complete with a wheel and kiln. Instantly feeling at ease, Nora explained that something in her heart told her that pottery could be her calling. She wanted to live life on her terms, work with her hands, learn a craft, and use her creativity to express herself. Trusting her instincts, she packed her belongings, withdrew from school, and headed to the Blue Ridge Mountains, eventually finding her way to Floyd, Virginia.

Floyd deserves a quick mention. Since moving to Roanoke, I've come to appreciate bluegrass music, even though I'm not a die-hard fan. Located 30 miles southwest of Roanoke, Floyd hosts a lively jamboree at the Floyd Country Store every Friday night. Weather permitting, musicians with fiddles, banjos, mandolins, and guitars line the sidewalks and join in the jam session. It's a unique experience, and I've never seen anything quite like it. Musicians play everything from gospel and Celtic to bluegrass, and somehow, it all feels just right with the world.

In the 1970s, Nora joined this vibrant mix of country musicians and the hippie wave already present in Floyd. The town is known for its high concentration of creative talent, from musicians to artists and potters. This is where Nora found her passion for pottery and, ultimately, the love of her life.

My new acquaintance didn't seem to mind that I was taking her time at the Market that Saturday and went on to tell me that it is never too late to make a change in your life. Nora was so enthusiastic in explaining how she enjoys living life on her terms, working with her hands, creating, having her time clock, meeting different people every week and supporting herself in what she refers to as a simple, pleasurable, happy, less stressful, fulfilling life. Nora reiterated to me as we were winding down our conversation and she was wrapping my mugs, "Remember, it's never ever too late to make a change in your life". Nora handed me my bag and said, "Your dreams are waiting for you." If that didn't give me a kickstart to my day! I walked away thinking of how courageous Nora was and had to have barriers and obstacles to overcome. However, Nora believed in herself and set her mind to learn a new skill to allow her to live life on her terms and live her dream on a vision and perhaps a prayer.

I've moved several times and feel that another geographic change is in the very near future and soon I will find my empty velvet hangers swaying in my closet, yet again. I'm choosing to think that Nora was put in my life path to help me think about reinventing myself in some way, shape or fashion, wherever my travels will take me. The possibilities are endless, and the world is out there waiting for me. Thanks, Nora, for being an inspiration and so interesting to talk to and for giving me much food for thought. I love thinking about the dreams that are waiting for me and it could be time to make them come true. I don't think I'll be performing blue grass music with a banjo; however, I was gifted a guitar and I'm seeing myself mastering a new skill, plucking one guitar string at a time. Crazier things have happened...you just never know.

OUR TURN MOM TO BE MOMCATS

My mother's kitchen has so many treasures that tell her life story dish by dish. Wooden salad bowls, the original Pyrex measuring cups, mixing bowls that were wedding gifts from 1953, Jello molds, cookie cutters that were my grandmothers, hand crank eggbeater and food mill, butter molds, egg coddler, tin pantry labeled bins for flour and sugar, hand carved dough bowls, recipe card boxes; you name it, and Big Kat has it. With the stocked cabinets mom is always telling us to take anything we want to help add space in her small but mighty kitchen. I thought this fat cat mug was clever and on one of my many trips to and from Ohio to Pennsylvania,

I borrowed this cup for my return trip to The Buckeye State and my mother told me to just keep and add the mug to my collection. I've always loved BKLIBAN's cats and the many sketches of the humorous felines, so I was delighted with my mom's suggestion.

BKLIBAN's mug caught my eye the other morning as I was making my daily coffee cup selection. It took me to thoughts of how my brother and me took/take turns in being the MOMCATS to our parents.

I noticed some changes in my father's behavior as he was in his winter years of his life. I attributed the actions to perhaps my father just being MW at times and aging. I have a friend that made a statement to me that is so simple, but it defines the process of aging along with the frustration, worry and concern in three words...THIS AGING THING. A lot comes along with THIS AGING THING and so much to be learned. I do not have a handbook on how to help with the shall we say antiquity, and I know I didn't have one for dementia in which my father so brilliantly masked for years.

My dad fell in June of 2008 and broke his hip and had to have surgery. The anesthesia from the procedure kicked his dementia into full gear and this dreadful disease took over my father. The silver lining in this part of my father's journey is that my brother was on break from school and was able to be there to spend time with him. We did a good job at being MOMCATS for our dad, but we also had my mom to help us and be the shining star. My mother always supported my father, and he was dependent upon her quiet strength to pull him through. We all were. We got through this time with many heartbreaks and disappointments, but we learned from the original and I feel as a family, we did right for my father as best we could. We became stronger, leaned on each other and tried to give my father all the love, dignity and respect that he deserved. We couldn't make my dad recover no matter what we did. All we could do was try to show our love for the best dad ever through smiles, laughs and many tears.

My father passed away in August of that same year. A Complete and devasting blow to me. I lost my biggest fan, cheerleader, man who loved me the most and one of my best friends. I was not the poster child on how to do Grief 101. I struggled and spent a good part of the year after losing my father drifting before I felt that I could come back amongst the living. There are some beautiful moments that occur during the leading up to the loss of a loved one, as crazy as this sounds, they do exist. Those moments are often recalled and shared fondly; I wouldn't trade them for the world. We did the best we could to provide solace for each other and give our best at being MOMCATS, being led by our mother's determination to make it all work and her understanding of the world as a whole and what we needed to do for our family.

The MOMCATS role is making a second appearance for my brother and me. The time has come for us to play the part for our mother; our beautiful, intelligent, talented, close to perfect mom. The toughest part of my life I have ever experienced. I'm sure this time is something my mother isn't quite fond of and finds it tough herself. However, I find myself learning new things about her in this season that somehow, I know she is going to do something to impress the hell out of me.

I'm very fortunate that Jeff does more than his fair share and I have learned that he has patience, kindness, compassion, attentiveness and a soft heart for making sure that our mom is going to be alright. I also have to say that I think Jeff is better at dealing with THIS AGING THING than I am.

I never thought that we would have to tag team and make decisions for our beacon in life. Our guide, backbone, rock and shining star. However, here we are trying to do everything we can to accommodate our mother and her wishes. It's a tough road and the decisions are not easy. Since we are in the throes of role reversals currently in our lives, I don't know the outcome, nor do I understand how everything is going to play out. I want all my mother's wishes to be granted. I never knew how hard this would be on my mind, body, spirit and soul. Perhaps, I'm to learn a thing or two about myself and this is a test to make me stronger and a better person, assume responsibility and give it my final try to grow up. I just don't know.

What I do know is I'm trying to do the best that I can, and right now, I feel that my best isn't good enough. I also know that I'm a lucky sister and I feel my big brother is the best one in the world. Maybe that's what I'm to learn and remember from this time in my life. For as much as Jeff and I have had our sibling spats and dramas, I've always loved him and have been proud of him. I couldn't imagine going through this time of MOMCATS with anyone else.

I guess I'll have to stay tuned to how everything unfolds and do a lot of praying. I pray that my best friend, my mom, knows I love her and admire her with all my heart, and that we are trying to do our very, very best at being MOMCATS. We learned from the best MOMCAT around and we owe it to her to do everything we can to repay her for all she did and still does for us.

I know most of us think they have the best mom in the world. My brother bought my mom a robe that reads "BEST MOM". My mother wears that soft, fluffy, white wrap with pride as she should as that is how we feel. I just hope our star knows how strong and deep our feelings run.

Please wish us luck and say a little prayer or two for OUR original, the one and only MOMCAT, otherwise known as THE BIG KAT my best girl and one of the two greatest people I have ever met.

CREATING A CONNECTION WITH THE POWER OF A THANK YOU

Alright, here we go again, this has all the makings of another MW Neal life lesson, but it is an important one to me and something I enjoy very much. The writing of a thank you note.

MWN had the most beautiful penmanship of anyone that I have ever known. Hands down my father's signature was so elegant, big and bold. I loved to watch him sign his name as his pen flowed with pride across any page or document he signed. The Big Guy should have had beautiful handwriting as that is how he started his career in the 1950's. My dad worked for Peterson Handwriting in Pennsylvania and drove from school-to-school teaching children printing and cursive writing. My father was teaching in Gettysburg PA and often had the secret service in his room as President Ike Eisenhower's grandson was one of his students. I always loved that story; however, I despised it when I was a pupil and had to sit at the kitchen table and practice. I can still hear my father's voice chanting, "round, round ready write" as I had to do the writing exercises. Dad loved and believed in handwriting so much that he developed his own patented cursive writing system.

My father was a stenographer in the Korean War as he was stationed in Sendai Japan. I have several of his notebooks that I flip through from time to time and think back on what it must've been like for my young, not yet father across the Pacific all those years ago. I don't recognize any of the symbols that my dad had to convert into words, phrases and sentences; However, they are beautiful testaments to my father's talent, and I love having these treasures. So, it goes without saying that handwriting was very much stressed in our family and along with that came learning about the power of a thank you note and the importance they play in our lives to make a connection and according to both of my parents, just good old fashion manners.

Anytime I go to my mailroom to collect our daily mail, the first item that I open is the envelope in which the address is handwritten. Bills, catalogues, magazines, direct advertising can all wait, bring on the personal cards and letters. I love to keep in touch with friends ACROSS THE MILES, and one of my favorite ways to do so is through correspondence. I like to create a connection with a thank you note to acknowledge and show my appreciation when a kindness, good deed or thoughtful gesture has been expressed and shared with me. I don't need anything in return, I just want to convey my gratefulness for someone thinking of me and taking the time to make my heart sing and let them know the impact that their efforts have made me feel. I know the ease with today's technology, texts, emails, social media are ways of thanking someone. I still prefer the old fashion way and love the beautiful and fun stationery and cards that are available to send with a stamp using the good old USPS. I grew up observing my parents writing thank you notes and my mother at the age of 95 still writes them today. My father wrote a thank you note to my high school bus driver for showing me kindness when my dog was hit by a car as I boarded the bus at the bottom of my driveway. The gentleman attended my father's funeral and expressed to me that my dad was the only one that ever thanked him for caring and keeping children safe over the years. The impact of a thank you takes a few minutes to create, the impression and feelings can last a lifetime. It's never too late for a thank you. Go ahead and make someone's day.

On that note, if you are reading this page, it means you have made it to the end of my book, and we are about to land at our destination. I can't tell you how much it means to me that you have taken the time to come along with me as I have checked a box on my bucket list.

I remember when my brother was writing his first book," What a Long Strange it's Been" by Dr. Jeffrey W. Neal (you can THANK me for the plug later Jeff). Jeff was sharing with me his feelings of the fear of the unknown and how challenging he was finding it to put his life out there for all to read in his written words. I remember telling Jeff, "Why do you care? Just go for it, enjoy and have fun". I wanted my brother to enjoy his significant accomplishment. That is easier said than done and I now completely understand my brother's pause and slight hesitation.

In my case of my life thoughts, not only am I the author if you will, but I'm also the editor; me, myself and I. My punctuation and grammar in my work hint to me that I may need to revisit English 101 or should've paid closer attention to Miss Savelli in High School, however, the work is mine even with all my hemming and hawing on my presentation of the English language.

So, when I type the words THANK YOU, I truly mean it and I'm humbled that you have taken the time to read my LIFE THOUGHTS… ONE CUP AT A TIME. Thank you, thank you, thank you for reading and sipping along.

PATS ON THE BACK

I started my project with my coffee mugs in late 2022. Now it is 2024. My best friend, my mother, and my aunt are no longer with me. I take comfort in the fact that those two Golden Girls are reunited once again. My Mom and Dad being together gives me a sense of peace as I live with a layer of sadness that I know will always be with me. I do love that the two sisters are also with their mother, father, sisters and my aunt is reunited with her husband, my unforgettable Uncle John. It does my shattered heart some good knowing that they are all together again. My Uncle Bun has also gone to the lofty heavens up above, so I smile imagining a lot of old fashions have been enjoyed over many rounds of three handed bridge games and political discussions.

When my mother passed away in October of 2023, I had all my thoughts for my project in motion, just not executed to a personal desired outcome for me. I decided to keep my collection in present tense and continue as my mother would've wanted me to do.

I'm thankful I was able to read most of my thoughts to my mother as we were seated at her dining room windows. Thank you, Mom, for being my biggest fan and cheerleader, you and Dad of course were co-captains in that field and your legacies will live on and I will do my best to make you both proud and keep sharing your stories. You made every day feel like Christmas.

I most importantly want to thank you mom and dad for giving me the gift of life and making me see the significance in every opportunity and pleasure in all the many life thoughts and moments. You both have taught me to have an enthusiastic awareness of life and prepared me to embrace all that it brings to me.

I'd like to thank Rustin for listening to me read my work at all hours of the day. I know he could recite this book in his sleep because he didn't miss a word of it. I appreciate the time that Rustin gave to me no matter how early in the morning I needed attention to help with the editing and a sounding board for my project. Truly not one complaint. Rustin of course was there 110% with his opinions and feedback that could at times result in let's just say discussions. The support was immeasurable and forever appreciated. I love us and the way we do life. It's an adventure and challenge for sure and I'm glad I hopped on the ride. And as I predicted, we left empty, velvet hangers swaying in our closets in Roanoke, and we found our way to a new adventure in Lake Geneva Wisconsin.

My illustrator has been drawing since he was 5 years of age. Thank you, Jon Ross, for tackling this project and making me feel like I needed to step up my writing game as your artwork and your interpretations of my words made me so proud of you once again. You are my star, and you make my heart shine and my life complete. Your contributions and talent are the best part of our endeavor. You truly have been my life saver.

It is so fun to have a Big Brother. Thank you, Jeffrey, for being the TOP MOM-CAT. You did more than your fair share to help Mom and Dad have the dignity that they deserved in their winter seasons. I think one of moms beaming life moments was to attend your first book signing. Thank you for making that possible for our Mama Bear, but of course you would, you will forever be the Golden Child. All kidding aside, you have been a wonderful son and the best big brother. I'm so proud of your book and you.

I don't know where I would be without the friends that are in my book. Not all were mentioned by name, but I know you can place yourselves in my life coffee thoughts. I love each one of you that is in my circle, and I'm beyond grateful for the laughs, tears, hugs, memories and life thoughts. The bonds of friendships keep me centered, focused and guide me to my True North. You have been for a long time my life forces, thank you.

Ty Roth, thank you for being a guide for my road to publishing when I didn't know where to turn. I love your statement to me, "Good on ya, Kitty"! My goal would not have been set in motion without your guidance, words and support, so back to you, "Good on ya, Ty"! Thank you.

And to you Kate, thank you for mailing mugs Across the Miles to give me the nudge to get me in motion with my writing journey. Thank you for believing in me more than I did myself and encouraging me to chase my idea. Your support has been inestimable.

Made in the USA
Columbia, SC
07 June 2025

2b36493b-a680-4db3-8b1b-c60d485e1547R02